Tyrannosaurus

A DK PUBLISHING BOOK
www.dk.com

Project editor Monica Byles
Art editor Penny Lamprell
Designer Peter Radcliffe
Managing art editor Chris Scollen
Managing editor Jane Yorke
Production Louise Bartrum and Neil Palfreyman

Research Mary Ann Lynch
Illustration Simone Boni/L. R. Galante
Tyrannosaurus **model** Graham High/Centaur Studios
Model photography Dave King
Museum photography Lynton Gardiner
UK Consultant Dr. Angela Milner, The Natural
History Museum, London
US Consultant Dr. Mark Norell, The American
Museum of Natural History, New York

First Paperback Edition, 1999
4 6 8 10 9 7 5 3
Published in the United States by
DK Publishing, Inc., 95 Madison Avenue
New York, NY 10016

The material is this book originally appeared in
Dinosaur Spotter's Guides: Tyrannosaurus published by Dorling Kindersley.

Published in Great Britain by Dorling Kindersley Limited
Library of Congress Cataloging-in-Publication Data

Lindsay, William. Tyrannosaurus / William Lindsay. – 1st American ed. p. cm.
Includes index. Summary: Describes the discovery and excavation of fossil evidence for the
Tyrannosaurus and examines what this evidence suggests about its appearance and behavior.
ISBN 0-7894-4272-8. 1. Tyrannosaurus rex – Juvenile literature. [1. Tyrannosaurus rex.
2. Dinosaurs. 3. Fossils. 4. Paleontology.] I. Title. QE862.S3L56 1999 567.9'7 dc20
92-52820 CIP AC

Color reproduction by Colourscan, Singapore
Printed and bound in Italy by Graphicom

AMERICAN MUSEUM OF NATURAL HISTORY

Tyrannosaurus

William Lindsay

Consultant Mark Norell

DK PUBLISHING, INC.
www.dk.com

CONTENTS

INTRODUCTION

About 230 million years ago an extraordinary group of animals appeared on Earth – dinosaurs. Dinosaurs were reptiles. They had scaly skins and laid eggs that had tough, waterproof shells. They lived only on land; there were no swimming or flying dinosaurs. These amazing creatures soon came to dominate life on land and remained supreme for more than 150 million years until their dramatic disappearance – an extinction that remains a mystery to this day.

Tyrannosaurus rex lived in western North America between 67 and 65 million years ago. It was one of the largest meat-eating animals that has ever lived on land, and one of the last dinosaurs to walk the Earth.

Fossil remains of *Tyrannosaurus rex* are rare. Apart from single teeth, fewer than twenty fossil specimens have been found, and only five or six of these are reasonably complete skeletons. One of the best finds of all, collected in 1908 by the famous American dinosaur hunter Barnum Brown, is featured in this book.

We have learned a great deal about *Tyrannosaurus rex's* lifestyle and its place in evolution from the careful study of its bones. We now know that it was not related to other large meat-eating dinosaurs but to advanced small meat-eaters like *Deinonychus* and *Troodon*, and that its closest living relatives are the birds. We also know what other kinds of dinosaurs shared its world.

However, the remains of *Tyrannosaurus rex* will never reveal what the living animal was really like. Paleontologists can only make educated guesses as to how it behaved, how fast it ran, and the color of its skin. Facts such as these remain a mystery, lost forever in the past.

Dr. Mark Norell
Chairman and Curator
Department of Vertebrate Paleontology
American Museum of Natural History, New York City

TYRANT LIZARD

*T*yrannosaurus rex is one of the most famous of all the dinosaurs. Even its name makes you imagine huge, nightmarish monsters. But *Tyrannosaurus* was no make-believe monster. Millions of years after its death, scientists are now able to piece together this great creature from its fossilized remains, providing some answers to many puzzling questions.

Scaly skin
Rare impressions of dinosaur skin have been found fossilized in ancient rocks. It was thick, tough, scaly, and waterproof, similar to that of modern-day reptiles, like the crocodile.

Tyrannosaurus rex
(Tie-ran-oh-saw-rus recks) means "king of the tyrant lizard." *Tyrannosaurus* means "tyrant lizard."

Two types of dinosaur
Dinosaurs are divided into two groups by the shape and position of their hip or pelvic bones. "Bird-hipped" or ornithischian dinosaurs were plant-eaters; their two lower hip bones pointed backwards and down to accommodate their large guts. "Lizard-hipped" or saurischian dinosaurs, such as *Tyrannosaurus rex,* were primarily meat-eaters and had shorter, less bulky guts, allowing their hip bones to sit closer together. One of their two lower hip bones pointed forwards and their other bone pointed backwards.

Heterodontosaurus "bird-hipped" dinosaur

Struthiomimus "lizard-hipped" dinosaur

Walking tall
Unlike most reptiles, whose legs sprawl out at the sides of their bodies, dinosaurs stood on legs held straight beneath their bodies. This enabled dinosaurs to move about more easily than other reptiles. Some dinosaurs walked on four legs. Others, such as *Tyrannosaurus rex,* walked on two.

Meat-eater

Carnivores (meat-eaters) such as *Tyrannosaurus rex* had sharp teeth and claws for slicing into flesh. *Tyrannosaurus rex* had extremely strong jaws that were powered by mighty muscles, enabling it to open its mouth so wide that it could have swallowed a human in just two bites!

FACT FILE

- **Lived:** 67-65 million years ago, during the late Cretaceous Period.

- **Family:** Tyrannosaurids, one of coelurosaurian group

- **Dinosaur type:** Lizard-hipped (saurischian)

- **Maximum life span:** Possibly up to 100 years

- **Diet:** Meat of dinosaurs and other animals

- **Weight when alive:** A little over 6 tons (up to 7 tonnes)

- **Height:** 18 ft (6m)

- **Length:** 42 ft (14 m)

- **Top speed:** Possibly up to 15 mph (25 km/h)

Like most two-legged predators, *Tyrannosaurus rex* could move quickly. However, *Tyrannosaurus* could probably not run at speed for long distances because of its great size.

Lost worlds

Dinosaur species appeared and died out over three periods of the Earth's history. *Tyrannosaurus* lived at the end of the Cretaceous Period.

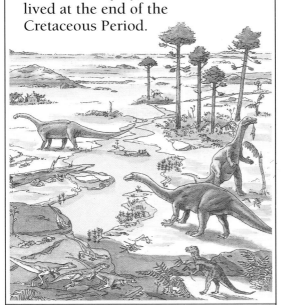

TRIASSIC PERIOD
248–205 million years ago

JURASSIC PERIOD
205–144 million years ago

CRETACEOUS PERIOD
144–65 million years ago

FOSSIL FINDS

The story of the death, fossilization, and discovery of one *Tyrannosaurus rex* spans more than 65 million years. When *Tyrannosaurus* died at the end of the Cretaceous Period, it was buried under sand and mud, where its skeleton was slowly fossilized.

In July 1908, Barnum Brown, one of America's greatest dinosaur hunters, spotted the exposed *Tyrannosaurus* fossil bones jutting out of rocks near Hell Creek, Montana. Eight years earlier, Brown had discovered the first unfamiliar remains of this new dinosaur species, later named *Tyrannosaurus rex*. But the second find was much more complete. This 1908 specimen is still used to identify new *Tyrannosaurus* fossil specimens today.

Journey through the earth
After its death around 65 million years ago, the body of this *Tyrannosaurus rex* was not destroyed by other animals. The skeleton survived intact in its rocky grave for millions of years, until earth movements and weathering exposed it once more.

Dry season
A long drought has dried up the lush swamps and forests. A few plants still grow along old riverbeds.

Wet season
Later in the year, heavy rains bring flash floods. Dead animals and plants are buried in sand and mud as the waters subside.

New life
Hundreds of years later, the river has changed course. Other dinosaurs now feed on the plants that grow by the river.

1 Alive and well
Tyrannosaurus prowls along drying riverbeds, where other dinosaurs gather to feed and drink.

2 Washed away
Killed by disease, attack, or drowning, *Tyrannosaurus* is carried off in floodwaters.

3 Dead and buried
Buried under sand and mud, only bones and teeth remain. The dinosaur's soft flesh has long since rotted away.

4 Turned to stone
The skeleton is now buried under many layers of rock. Chemicals have slowly changed the bones into hard fossils.

5 Inside the Earth
Movements deep below the Earth's crust force the *Tyrannosaurus* skeleton closer to the surface. The fossil bones are now cracked and broken.

Terrible tooth
Dinosaur teeth are often well-preserved as fossils, because they are hard and resistant to decay. A *Tyrannosaurus* tooth may be as long as 7 in (18 cm), with a sharp, serrated edge for cutting and tearing the flesh of its prey.

In the footsteps of Barnum Brown

The rocks of Hell Creek, Montana, were formed in the Late Cretaceous Period of the Earth's history. They belong to the time of the last dinosaurs and today are scoured for treasures by fossil hunters.

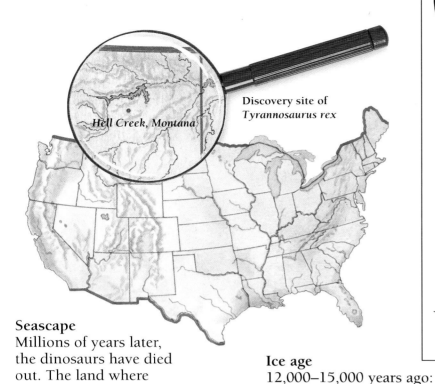

Hell Creek, Montana

Discovery site of *Tyrannosaurus rex*

Seascape

Millions of years later, the dinosaurs have died out. The land where they once lived is now covered by sea.

Ice age

12,000–15,000 years ago: the sea has long gone and the land is now frozen. Earth movements have pushed up mountains.

6 Into daylight

The rock of the ancient riverbed has been carved by wind and rain into hills and canyons. Weathering has finally brought the *Tyrannosaurus* fossils back to the surface.

DIGGING FOR DINOSAURS

Plaster jacket containing fossil

Like many dinosaur discoveries, the *Tyrannosaurus rex* specimen of 1908 was found in desolate, open country, far from the nearest settlement. Barnum Brown and his field team set up camp in the badlands of Montana, five days' travel by horsedrawn wagon from the nearest railway.

The excavation took three months of backbreaking work. Some of the *Tyrannosaurus* bones were easily removed from sand, but others were buried in rock as hard as granite. Scrapers, picks, shovels, and even dynamite were used to free the fossil bones.

Materials needed to make a plaster jacket

Chisels for chipping rock

Burlap

1 Excavating the fossils
Once rubble had been cleared from around the skeleton, the fossil hunters carefully began to chip rock away from the individual bones. When the fragile fossils were exposed, they were then strengthened with glue and wrapped in burlap soaked in plaster of Paris.

2 Shipping the fossils
Once the protective plaster jacket had dried, each fossil could be removed from site. The fossils were hoisted into wooden crates. Each heavy crate was hauled by horse and cart to the railway, some 150 miles (240 km) away from the excavation site.

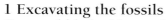

Missing or fragile bones, like those of the skull, were modeled in plaster.

3 Studying the fossils
At the Museum in New York, the plaster jackets were removed and the delicate fossils carefully restored. The bones were then compared with those of other *Tyrannosaurus* finds. At last, the complete dinosaur skeleton could be carefully pieced together.

4 Skeleton display

In 1915, the scientists began to prepare the original fossils for a new museum display. Ropes and pulleys held all the heavy bones in place while the mount was built.

A lighter plaster cast was hung in place of the fragile, heavy skull.

Ropes held all the bones securely in position, while the supporting metal framework was built around the fossil skeleton.

The dinosaur builders worked from wooden platforms, laid across scaffolding, high above the Museum floor.

Trowel for mixing plaster

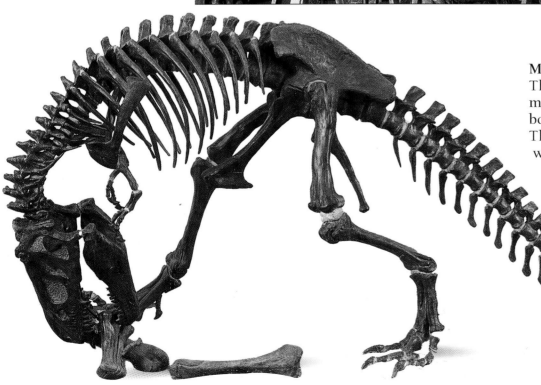

Mini-dinosaurs

The dinosaur builders made detailed scale models, one-sixth of life size, showing every bone in the skeleton of *Tyrannosaurus rex*. These models helped the scientists to experiment with different display positions for their fullsize mount. The model shown here demonstrates how *Tyrannosaurus rex* might have been mounted, gnawing on a carcass.

RECONSTRUCTING TYRANNOSAURUS

The *Tyrannosaurus rex* skeleton found by Barnum Brown was put on display at the American Museum of Natural History in 1915, seven years after its discovery. The new mount was over 42 ft (14 m) long and stood nearly 18 ft (over 5 m) tall. *Tyrannosaurus* is easily recognized by its large skull and rib cage, long legs and tail, and by its strange, small arms. Scientists have puzzled over how the dinosaur might have used its arms. They probably would not have been helpful for feeding because they were too short to reach its mouth!

Long jaws lined with meat-slicing, serrated teeth

Front view
Seen from the front, 65 million years after its death, *Tyrannosaurus rex* is still a terrifying example of the carnivorous dinosaurs.

Correct position with tail held up off the ground

Tiny arms have two clawed fingers on each hand.

The rib cage is deep at the front, but narrows toward the rear. The ribs curve inward to protect the soft organs in the body cavity.

Corrected reconstruction
Carnosaurs, the family of large meat-eating dinosaurs like *Tyrannosaurus rex,* walked on two legs, not four. However, when the *Tyrannosaurus* skeleton was first reconstructed, it was shown with its tail resting on the ground and its body held upright. Scientists now believe that the living dinosaur held its body almost level with the ground, balanced by its tail held in the air.

Tail vertebrae

Towering monster
If *Tyrannosaurus* were alive today, it would tower above most living land animals, including people.

Bones of the feet were locked together for strength.

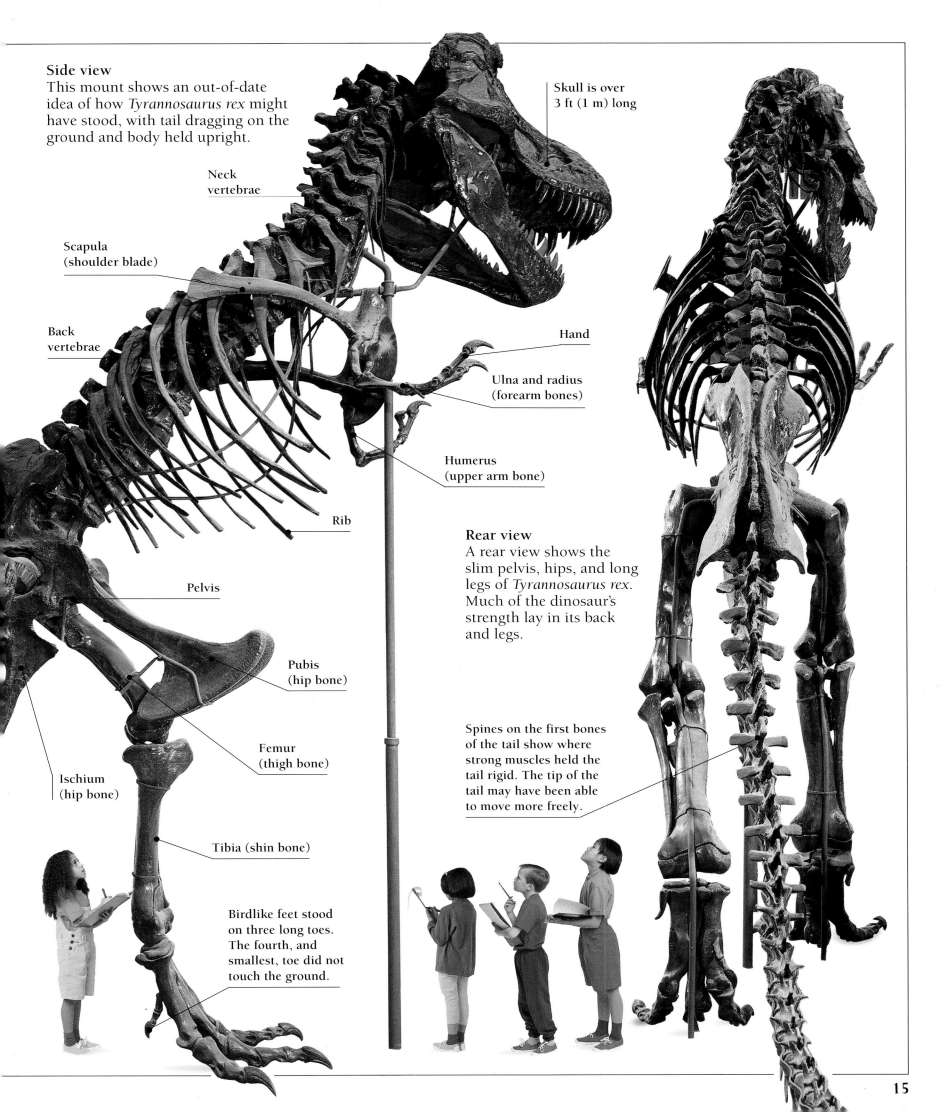

Side view
This mount shows an out-of-date idea of how *Tyrannosaurus rex* might have stood, with tail dragging on the ground and body held upright.

Neck vertebrae

Skull is over 3 ft (1 m) long

Scapula (shoulder blade)

Back vertebrae

Hand

Ulna and radius (forearm bones)

Humerus (upper arm bone)

Rib

Rear view
A rear view shows the slim pelvis, hips, and long legs of *Tyrannosaurus rex*. Much of the dinosaur's strength lay in its back and legs.

Pelvis

Pubis (hip bone)

Femur (thigh bone)

Ischium (hip bone)

Spines on the first bones of the tail show where strong muscles held the tail rigid. The tip of the tail may have been able to move more freely.

Tibia (shin bone)

Birdlike feet stood on three long toes. The fourth, and smallest, toe did not touch the ground.

MUSCLE POWER

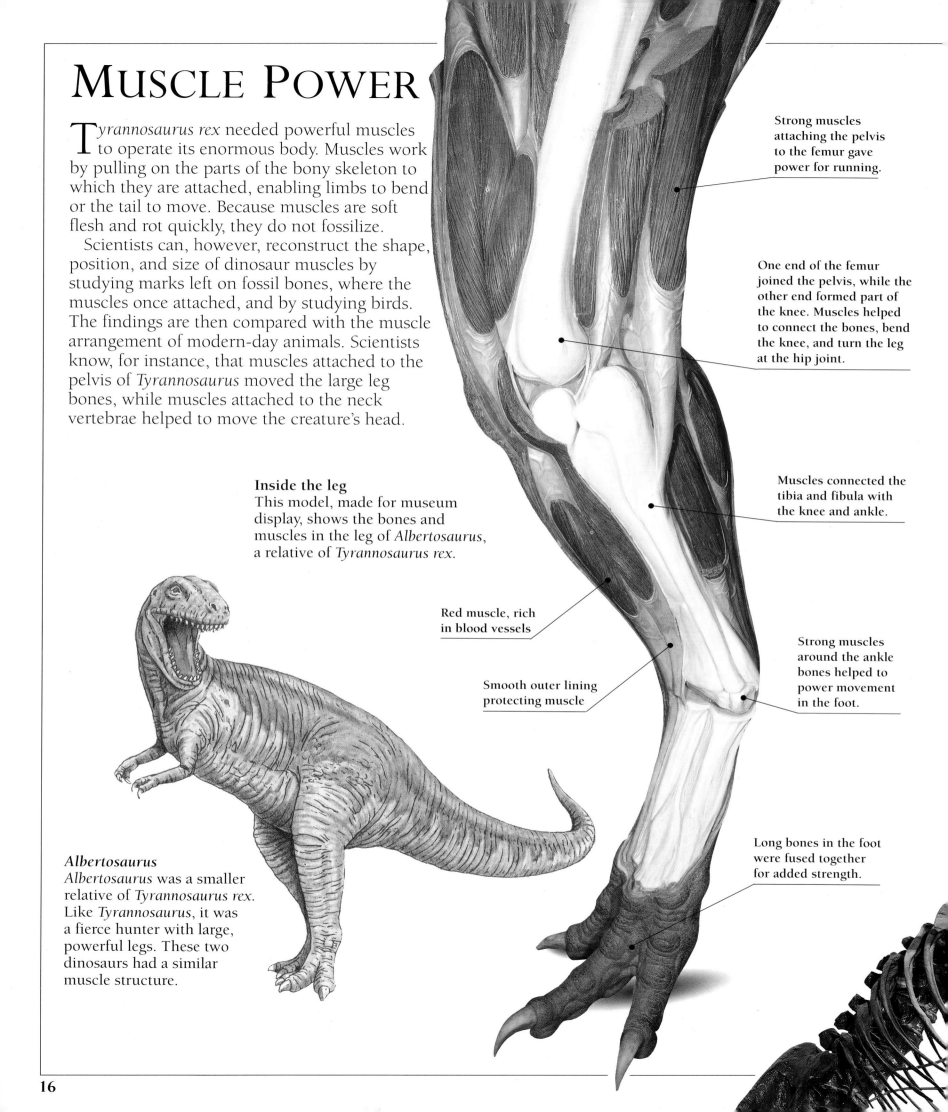

Tyrannosaurus rex needed powerful muscles to operate its enormous body. Muscles work by pulling on the parts of the bony skeleton to which they are attached, enabling limbs to bend or the tail to move. Because muscles are soft flesh and rot quickly, they do not fossilize.

Scientists can, however, reconstruct the shape, position, and size of dinosaur muscles by studying marks left on fossil bones, where the muscles once attached, and by studying birds. The findings are then compared with the muscle arrangement of modern-day animals. Scientists know, for instance, that muscles attached to the pelvis of Tyrannosaurus moved the large leg bones, while muscles attached to the neck vertebrae helped to move the creature's head.

Strong muscles attaching the pelvis to the femur gave power for running.

One end of the femur joined the pelvis, while the other end formed part of the knee. Muscles helped to connect the bones, bend the knee, and turn the leg at the hip joint.

Muscles connected the tibia and fibula with the knee and ankle.

Inside the leg
This model, made for museum display, shows the bones and muscles in the leg of Albertosaurus, a relative of Tyrannosaurus rex.

Red muscle, rich in blood vessels

Strong muscles around the ankle bones helped to power movement in the foot.

Smooth outer lining protecting muscle

Long bones in the foot were fused together for added strength.

Albertosaurus
Albertosaurus was a smaller relative of Tyrannosaurus rex. Like Tyrannosaurus, it was a fierce hunter with large, powerful legs. These two dinosaurs had a similar muscle structure.

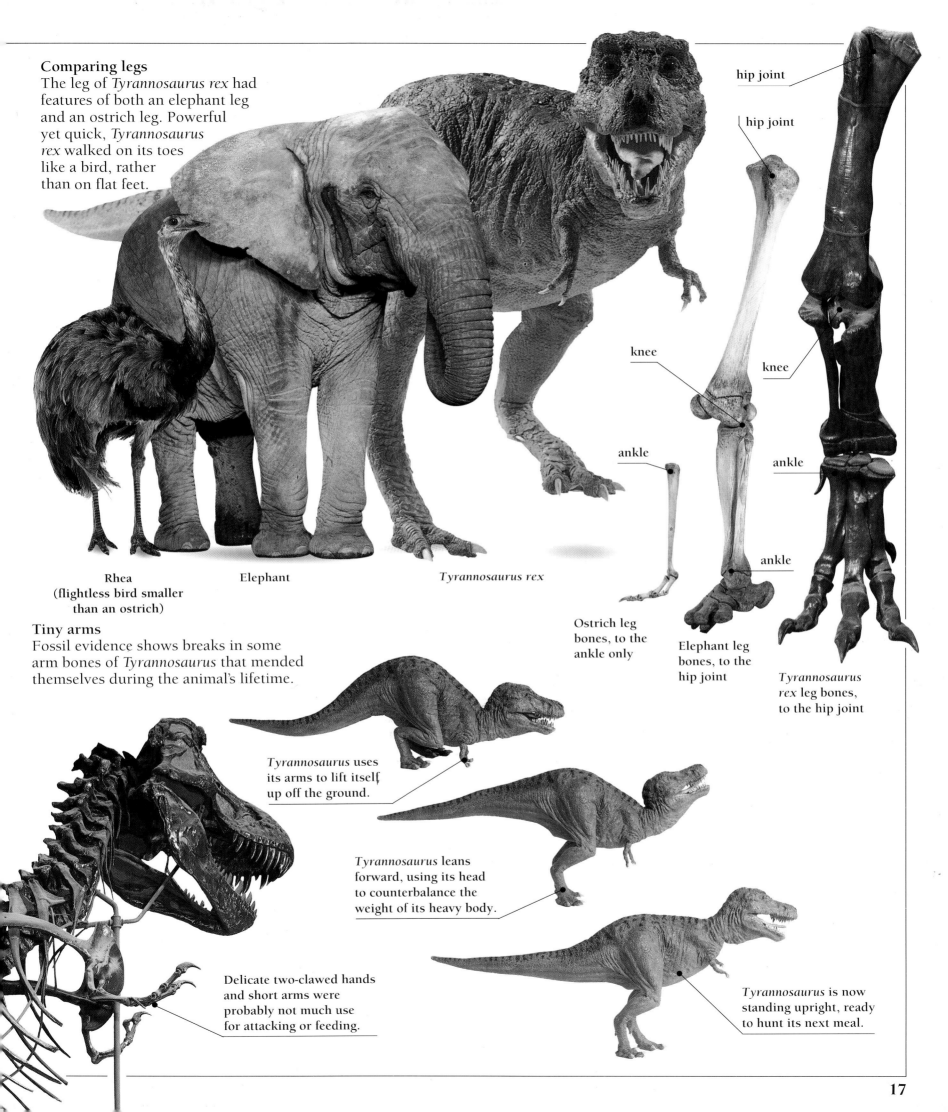

Comparing legs

The leg of *Tyrannosaurus rex* had features of both an elephant leg and an ostrich leg. Powerful yet quick, *Tyrannosaurus rex* walked on its toes like a bird, rather than on flat feet.

hip joint

hip joint

knee

knee

ankle

ankle

ankle

Rhea
(flightless bird smaller
than an ostrich)

Elephant

Tyrannosaurus rex

Ostrich leg
bones, to the
ankle only

Elephant leg
bones, to the
hip joint

*Tyrannosaurus
rex* leg bones,
to the hip joint

Tiny arms

Fossil evidence shows breaks in some arm bones of *Tyrannosaurus* that mended themselves during the animal's lifetime.

Tyrannosaurus uses its arms to lift itself up off the ground.

Tyrannosaurus leans forward, using its head to counterbalance the weight of its heavy body.

Delicate two-clawed hands and short arms were probably not much use for attacking or feeding.

Tyrannosaurus is now standing upright, ready to hunt its next meal.

MONSTER IN MOTION

Tyrannosaurus rex was a ferocious hunter of dinosaurs and other animals. It had a massive head and a sturdy neck that could deliver a deadly and crushing blow to its prey. *Tyrannosaurus* used its strong toes and sharp claws to hold down its victims, while its vicious teeth sliced into their flesh. Few animals could escape a *Tyrannosaurus* on the attack.

Speeding dinosaur
Some scientists believe that a charging *Tyrannosaurus* could reach a top speed of over 15 mph (25 km/h). Other experts claim it was capable of running at up to 40 mph (64 km/h), as fast as a modern white rhino.

3 Spotting prey
Tyrannosaurus sights a young dinosaur, grazing apart from its herd. *Tyrannosaurus* turns its head for a better view.

Tyrannosaurus rex had strong legs tucked under its bulky body, which supported its 6 ton (7 tonne) weight.

2 On the prowl
Tyrannosaurus moves forward, swinging powerful legs under its huge body.

8 Deadly bite
The knife-sharp fangs of *Tyrannosaurus rex* close in on its next meal. One swift bite to the neck slices through blood vessels and windpipe and crushes bone.

1 Hungry hunter
A hungry *Tyrannosaurus* hunts for a likely victim. Its keen senses are ready to detect the presence of another predator that might steal its kill.

As it moved along, *Tyrannosaurus* used its long tail to counterbalance the weight of its massive body.

5 On the attack
Now in full attack, *Tyrannosaurus* charges forward toward its prey.

4 Ready to strike
Sweeping its muscular tail around, *Tyrannosaurus* moves in for the kill. If its strike is unsuccessful, *Tyrannosaurus* will have wasted vital energy and alerted the herd of grazing dinosaurs to danger.

7 In for the kill
Tyrannosaurus lunges forward with open jaws to catch its prey.

6 Towering tyrant
Tyrannosaurus throws up its head and roars. Rearing overhead, *Tyrannosaurus* is a terrifying sight to its victim.

GIANT JAWS

*T*yrannosaurus rex had one of the biggest and strongest heads of all the dinosaurs. This ferocious meat-eater could kill its prey with one crushing bite of its giant saber-toothed jaws, and then a twist of its powerful neck could tear away the first mouthful of meat. Even the tough, bony plates that shielded plant-eating dinosaurs of the time would have been savaged by *Tyrannosaurus'* immensely strong jaws and daggerlike fangs. Like other meat-eating dinosaurs, *Tyrannosaurus* was able to grow new teeth to replace those that were broken or worn down.

Skull discovery
The *Tyrannosaurus* skull shown here, found by Barnum Brown in Hell Creek, Montana, in 1908, is over 3 ft (1 m) long. Features such as the massive skull and jaw bones made it possible for *Tyrannosaurus* to swallow smaller dinosaurs whole.

A front view of the skull shows the huge bones, slightly crushed by fossilization

Openings for the air passages to the nostril

Scientists have left some of the rock between the bones to support the shape of the heavy skull.

The giant, serrated teeth curve backward, designed to grip and rip apart carcasses. The teeth form a deep cutting edge as they increase in size from the front to the middle of the jaws.

New teeth grew to replace those that were old and worn.

Fine holes along the margin of the jaws show where blood vessels passed out of the bone to the skin.

The deep, strong lower jaw had a large area of bone where the jaw muscles attached.

Bone-crusher
Tyrannosaurus rex had enormous and powerful jaws, operated by thick masses of muscle. Other dinosaurs could make their mouths larger by flexing their skull bones at special joints, just as some reptiles do today.

Small bony crest
on the roof of
the skull

Eye socket

Muscles from the neck
connected to the wide
area of bone at the
back of the skull.

Spaces between the
skull bones made the
head lighter and left
room for muscles.

Powerful neck
Strong neck muscles supported
Tyrannosaurus' mighty skull.
Tyrannosaurus could move
its head in all directions,
which helped it hold
down struggling prey.

Tyrannosaurus rex may have
had better-positioned eyes for
hunting than other dinosaurs.
Forward-facing eyes helped
it keep its prey in sight
as it charged.

Skin covering a
special area of skull
at the side of the
animal's head formed
Tyrannosaurus' ear.

Its thick, large
tongue helped
Tyrannosaurus
process its food
before swallowing.

KILLER INSTINCT

Tyrannosaurus rex was an animal well adapted for hunting. Bigger than any of the other meat-eating dinosaurs of its time, a 7 ton (8 tonne) *Tyrannosaurus* was powerful enough to attack even a 6 ton (6 tonne) heavily armored *Triceratops*. Its giant size was matched by an enormous appetite, and *Tyrannosaurus* seized every opportunity for catching a passing meal – the bigger the kill, the less hunting it had to do.

Tyrannosaurus was equipped with excellent tools for hunting and killing. In addition to the dinosaur's great size, strength, and fearsome teeth, it probably had good senses for seeing, hearing, and smelling its prey.

Staying alive
Like all animals, *Tyrannosaurus rex* had to eat to live. Although it may have stolen kills made by smaller carnivores, *Tyrannosaurus* was better equipped than most to hunt its own prey.

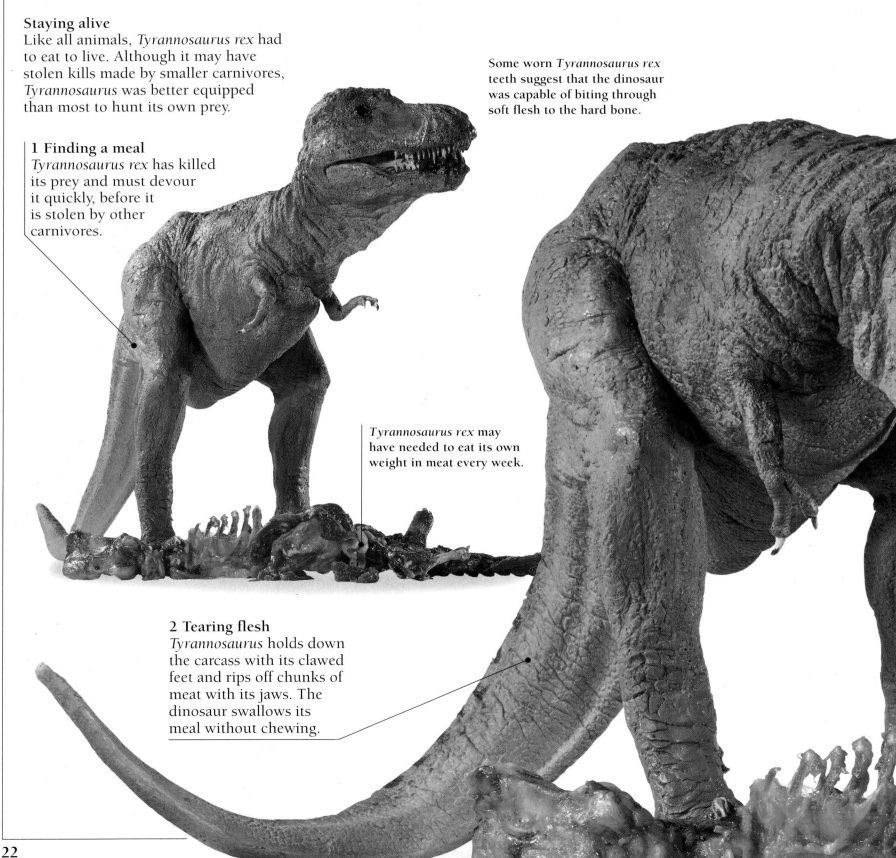

Some worn *Tyrannosaurus rex* teeth suggest that the dinosaur was capable of biting through soft flesh to the hard bone.

1 Finding a meal
Tyrannosaurus rex has killed its prey and must devour it quickly, before it is stolen by other carnivores.

Tyrannosaurus rex may have needed to eat its own weight in meat every week.

2 Tearing flesh
Tyrannosaurus holds down the carcass with its clawed feet and rips off chunks of meat with its jaws. The dinosaur swallows its meal without chewing.

Focusing on prey

Many dinosaurs had eyes at the sides of their head and saw a different view from each eye. Some animals, such as humans, have eyes that face forward and can form a single view. This lets them judge distances accurately.

Tyrannosaurus rex may have had eyes that faced forward, which helped it spot prey. No one knows if *Tyrannosaurus* saw in tones of gray or in color.

Single view from forward-facing eyes in color and in black and white

Double view from sideways-facing eyes in color and in black and white

Birdlike feet pinned the carcass to the ground.

Teeth were curved and serrated, designed to slice huge chunks of meat from the carcass.

3 Facing the competition
A second hungry *Tyrannosaurus* approaches, desperate to share in the kill. *Tyrannosaurus* prepares to defend its meal, and roars in an effort to frighten away its rival.

23

FEROCIOUS FIGHTER

Tyrannosaurus rex was the top predator living in North America in the Late Cretaceous period. Like lions today, Tyrannosaurus preyed on the plant-eating animals in its area. But unlike lions, which hunt in packs, Tyrannosaurus rex probably hunted alone.

Skeletons of large carnivores like Tyrannosaurus rex are usually found singly, not in groups. In one part of Canada, only five out of 100 dinosaur finds have been large meat-eaters. Tyrannosaurus may have needed to eat a lot of dinosaur meat to satisfy its huge appetite.

Face to face
Although most animals will try to avoid a fight, they may attack one another over food. Few dinosaurs would have risked attacking Tyrannosaurus rex. One Tyrannosaurus skull with damaged bones suggests, however, that another Tyrannosaurus might have tried, perhaps to steal a kill.

A face-to-face struggle between two hungry Tyrannosaurus would have been one of the most fearsome battles ever.

Gaping jaws
The tooth-lined jaws of Tyrannosaurus rex were its main weapons. Its mouth and fierce roar might have scared another animal off without a fight.

Deadly dance
Tyrannosaurus challenges, shifting and dodging to show off its strength and size. This display may frighten the rival away.

Ready to charge
The massive, muscular legs are ready to carry Tyrannosaurus in a headlong charge at its enemy, if it finally has to fight for its meal.

Cretaceous hunting ground
Tyrannosaurus would have preyed on many species of dinosaur. Most would have kept their distance from such a ferocious predator.

Safety in numbers
Triceratops, one of the most common dinosaurs of the period, grazed in herds for protection.

Saurolophus

Edmontosaurus

Ornithomimus

Parasaurolophus

Ankylosaurus

Fast runners
Duck-billed dinosaurs, like *Saurolophus*, *Edmontosaurus*, and *Parasaurolophus*, as well as the fast-running *Ornithomimus*, feed nervously as the fight continues. At the first sign of danger, they will escape into the safety of the forest.

Armored defense
An armored *Ankylosaurus* backs away from battle. Even with its powerful, muscular tail club, the animal prefers to avoid any danger.

Safe in the river
River turtles have picked clean the carcass of a dead dinosaur. Swept there by last season's floodwaters, the skeleton is now left half-buried in the silted shallows of the stream.

Swinging tails
Tails raised for balance, the two dinosaurs shift position to catch one another off guard.

TYRANNOSAURUS SPECIMEN AND FAMILY FACTS

- **Specimen number:** AMNH 5027
- **Excavated by:** Barnum Brown
- **Excavation:** 1908, at Hell Creek, Montana
- **Bones found:** Almost complete skeleton; missing the forelimbs and some leg bones which were modeled in plaster

- **Where displayed:** American Museum of Natural History, New York City*
- **First constructed:** 1915; made up primarily from original fossil bones; ropes and pulleys used during construction to hold all heavy bones in place

🏛 ON THE MUSEUM TRAIL 🏛

A museum guide to tyrannosaur specimens
A partial listing of both fossils and replica casts of fossils.

UNITED STATES
(*Tyrannosaurus*) University of Michigan Exhibit Museum, Ann Arbor, Michigan
(*Tyrannosaurus*) University of California, Museum of Paleontology, Berkeley, California
(*Tyrannosaurus*) Museum of the Rockies, Bozemann, Montana
(*Albertosaurus*) Field Museum of Natural History, Chicago, Illinois
(*Nanotyrannus*) Natural History Museum, Cleveland, Ohio
(*Tyrannosaurus*) Denver Museum of Natural History, Denver, Colorado
(*Tyrannosaurus*) The Museum, Michigan State University, East Lansing, Michigan

Carnosaur specimens may also be found in museums in Australia, Canada, France, Germany, Japan, Mongolia, Poland, Russia, Spain, Sweden, and the United Kingdom.

Dinosaur display
This is the specimen found by Brown in 1908. It was the first *Tyrannosaurus* skeleton ever built. It towered over other dinosaurs in the halls of the AMNH for many years.

(*Tyrannosaurus*)
   Los Angeles County Museum of Natural History, Los Angeles, California
(*Albertosaurus, Tyrannosaurus*)
   American Museum of Natural History, New York, New York
(*Tyrannosaurus*) Carnegie Museum of Natural History, Pittsburgh, Pennsylvania
(*Albertosaurus, Tyrannosaurus*) National Museum of Natural History, Smithsonian Institution,

Tyrannosaurus rex lived about 65 million years ago, at the end of the Cretaceous Period. It was one of the last dinosaurs.

*AMNH 5027 was completely remounted in a new pose for the revised AMNH dinosaur gallery opened in 1996.

Tyrannosaurus relatives
Tyrannosaurus and its fellow tyrannosaurids, *Albertosaurus* and *Tarbosaurus*, belong to a group of advanced meat-eaters called coelurosaurs. They are in turn related to *Allosaurus*, a tetanuran, and to ceratosaurs, such as *Ceratosaurus* and *Dilophosaurus*, which were a group of large early meat-eaters. All of these groups together form part of the larger group of theropods.

Ceratosaurus lived 150 million years ago in the Jurassic Period. It was less than half the size of *Tyrannosaurus rex*.

Albertosaurus was smaller than *Tyrannosaurus rex*. It lived in the Cretaceous Period and has been found in North America.

Dilophosaurus lived 200 million years ago, in the Early Jurassic Period. It was less than half the size of *Tyrannosaurus*.

Tarbosaurus was very similar to *Tyrannosaurus rex* but slightly smaller. Its remains have been found in Mongolia.

Allosaurus was a common hunter of 150 million years ago, in the Jurassic Period. Its fossils have been found in North America.

Worlds apart
Dinosaur remains have been found on every continent. New species of dinosaurs evolved and adapted over millions of years as climates and landscapes changed. This map shows areas where *Tyrannosaurus* and other theropods have been found.

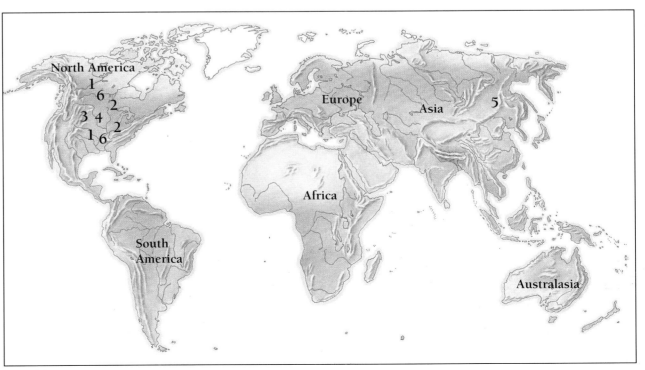

Key to map

1 *Albertosaurus*
2 *Allosaurus*
3 *Ceratosaurus*
4 *Dilophosaurus*
5 *Tarbosaurus*
6 *Tyrannosaurus*

GLOSSARY

carcass
The dead body of an animal.

carnivore
A meat-eating animal.

carnosaurs
A group of dinosaurs that were the largest meat-eaters to have lived on land.

Cretaceous Period
Part of the Earth's history that lasted from 144 million years ago until the dinosaurs died out 65 million years ago. *Tyrannosaurus rex* lived during this period.

dinosaurs
A group of extinct, land-living reptiles that lived on Earth from 230 to 65 million years ago.

environment
The land, water, and climate that surrounds living things and affects how they live.

excavate
To dig up an object such as a fossil.

extinction
When living things, such as dinosaurs, die out and disappear from the Earth forever.

formation
An arrangement of rock layers formed over millions of years.

fossil
Part of a dead plant or animal that has been buried and turned as hard as stone by chemicals in the rock.

herbivore
A plant-eating animal.

impression
A copy of the shape and surface markings of a fossil.

Jurassic Period
Part of the Earth's history from 205 to 144 million years ago, when large plant-eating sauropod dinosaurs were common.

organ
A soft part inside an animal's body, such as the heart or stomach.

ornithischian dinosaur
The bird-hipped type of dinosaur with both lower hip bones pointing down and backward.

paleontologist
A scientist who studies fossils and life in ancient times.

pelvis
A group of bones where the legs join the backbone.

predator
An animal that hunts and kills other animals to eat.

reptile
A scaly animal that lays shelled eggs, such as the turtles, snakes, lizards, and crocodiles of today. Dinosaurs were reptiles.

saurischian dinosaur
The lizard-hipped type of dinosaur with one of the two lower hip bones pointing down and forward and the other bone pointing down and backward.

scavenger
A meat-eater that feeds on prey that is already dead, rather than on prey that it has killed.

skeleton
The supporting bony frame inside an animal's body.

specimen
Something that is collected or preserved as an example from a particular group.

theropods
All meat-eating lizard-hipped dinosaurs, such as *Tyrannosaurus rex*.

Triassic Period
Part of the Earth's history, which lasted from 248 to 205 million years ago, during which the dinosaurs first appeared.

type specimen
The one specimen of an animal or plant that is used as a standard to compare with other specimens.

tyrannosaur
Best-known family within the carnosaurs.

vertebrae
Bones that form the backbone of animals.

weathering
When rocks and soil are broken up and washed or blown away by wind, rain, sun, frost, and other features of the weather.

Pronunciation guide to the dinosaur names in this book

- *Albertosaurus*
  (al-bert-oh-saw-rus)
- *Allosaurus*
  (al-low-saw-rus)
- *Ankylosaurus*
  (ank-kye-low-saw-rus)
- *Ceratosaurus*
  (seratto-saw-rus)
- *Daspletosaurus*
  (dass-pleet-oh-saw-rus)
- *Deinonychus*
  (die-non-e-cus)
- *Dilophosaurus*
  (dye-loff-oh-saw-rus)
- *Edmontosaurus*
  (ed-mon-toe-saw-rus)
- *Heterodontosaurus*
  (het-ter-row-dont-oh-saw-rus)
- *Ornithomimus*
  (ornith-oh-meem-us)
- *Parasaurolophus*
  (para-saw-rol-oh-fus)
- *Saurolophus*
  (saw-rol-oh-fus)
- *Struthiomimus*
  (strewth-ee-yo-meem-us)
- *Tarbosaurus*
  (tar-bow-saw-rus)
- *Triceratops*
  (try-ser-rah-tops)
- *Troodon*
  (tru-oh-don)
- *Tyrannosaurus rex*
  (tie-ran-oh-saw-rus recks)

INDEX

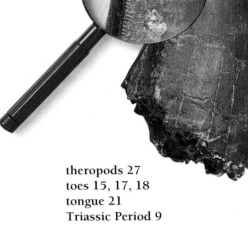
ACKNOWLEDGMENTS

Picture credits:
t=top b=bottom m=middle l=left r=right
Courtesy Department of Library Services,
American Museum of Natural History: Neg. no.
37243, 11tr; Neg. no. 335782, 11mr; Neg. no.
18338, 12tl; Neg. no. 18341, 12mr; Neg. no.
121779, 12b; Neg. no. 35923, 13tr; Neg. no.
121779, 28br.
    Model photography by Dave King 6bl, 7,
15ml, 17t, 17br, 18, 19, 21–25, 29ml, 29br.
Museum photography by Lynton Gardiner 13br,
14r, 15, 16br, 17tr, 20ml, 20/21m, 26mr, 28bl.
Additional special photography by Paul Bricknell
(magnifying glass) 10tl, 29tr; Andy Crawford 4,
5, 6tl, 6tr, 15bl, 26b; John Down 16r; Philip
Dowell (ostrich leg bone); Tim Ridley 12tr;
Harry Taylor 10bl, 29tr; Jerry Young 8tr, 17tl.

Dorling Kindersley would like to
thank Mandy Earey, Jonathan Buckley,
and Sharon Peters for their help in
producing this book.
    Thanks also to Jennie Joannides,
Natalie Ebrey, Jamie Ross, Darren
Chin, and Daniel Ray for
appearing in this book.
    Index by Lynn Bresler.